Marfa

Modern

HELEN THOMPSON

Marfa   Modern

Artistic Interiors

of the

West Texas

High Desert

Photographs by Casey Dunn

THE MONACELLI PRESS

On Marfa

They say everything can be replaced,
yet every distance is not near.
—Bob Dylan

Something magical happens each time I reach the twenty-six-mile stretch of highway between Alpine and Marfa. Perhaps it is the gradual softening of the landscape as it turns from rugged tundra to silvery, grass-covered hills, or it might be the boundless charm of the high desert, or perhaps it is the liberating sense of not wanting anything more than what the windshield can frame. Even after the almost ten-hour drive from Houston, those last few miles always produce a sudden desire to slow down, to delay my impending arrival—especially when it happens to coincide with a westward-bound train. A particular feeling of happiness overtakes me as I follow the uninterrupted flow of the train piercing the horizon, oblivious of the beauty it traverses, ignorant of the gentle or furious clouds that salute its path. There are few places on earth where an arrival can unfold in such charged slow motion across an ever-willing horizon. Sometimes I have had to stop so I could listen to a fleeting rain break away from a mutiny of clouds; I have

paused by the side of the road to watch the thinnest of clouds needle through an immovable Cathedral Mountain. Just like the many times I have lingered in the living room of one of the houses featured in these pages, watching other trains as they appear as distant yellow lines threading across the Davis Mountains, back and forth, in ceremonial silence.

Ever since my first visit to Marfa, in 1993, I have continued to experience many magical moments there. That first visit did not come about in search of Marfa's mesmerizing landscape, but rather to write about the works of Donald Judd for an architectural journal. More specifically, it was to report on Judd's visionary transformation of the dilapidated Fort D. A. Russell into the Chinati Foundation. At the time of my visit Judd was still living, the former military base seemed to be in a state of animated construction, and visitors were allowed to wander freely across the grounds. I recall casually peeking into one of the barracks, where I caught Ilya Kabakov in the midst of installing his work *School No. 6.* I had no inkling at the time who he was or what that particular work was all about. Nor did I know then that I would return to the Chinati Foundation many times over, that I would get to build in Marfa, or that I would conduct design studios based on Marfa subjects with students from Rice University—let alone that each subsequent trip from Houston to Marfa would usher in a renewed sense of anticipation and wonder.

Marfa is a place I know well now, having spent countless hours under its singular, limitless skies where all dilations of time are possible. Time measured by light acquires qualities and dimensions that words or photographs can only partially render. One recent morning when I was about to start the drive back to Houston, the breaking dawn—coming after a night of rain—covered the entire sky in trembling fireworks of color. Along Highland Avenue the buildings welcomed the explosive light as if for the first time: the same light that punctually arrives each day with its new and immemorial glow, the same light that quietly inhabits each house featured in this publication.

Architecture is a means of being in the world, of living in a place and discovering the subtleties of its limits. Architecture is also a means of transcending those limits as space unravels the rituals of light and the pleasures of time. Marfa is a marvelous setting to build in; any construction there becomes an essential timepiece, marking individual or collective stakes in the vast landscape. It does not matter if it concerns a modest adobe house or a tiny bungalow with oversized porches, an enormous soaring metal roof or a large window against the open view, a partially shaded courtyard or a precise corner where two streets meet. Each construction is a window in time, an opportunity to lessen the fraught velocity of our frenzied times; times soon forgotten or rendered barely audible against the incomparable beauty of the desert.

Carlos Jiménez
Professor of Architecture, Rice University

Preface

This book is as personal to me and Casey Dunn as the homes featured in these pages are personal to their owners—and I hope just as unique. Marfa, Texas, has always been exceptional and is becoming known as a place that welcomes and fosters particular opinions on how to live, but it thrives today in large part because artist Donald Judd decided to settle in the West Texas ranching town in 1971. The isolation, the landscape, and the sky were major factors that lured Judd to the high desert. His decision at the time was regarded as strange if not merely atypical, an idiosyncratic quest by an artist known for his antisocial tendencies. Now we think of Judd as prescient. He died in 1994, but the rigorously minimal, site-specific art for which he crusaded has never been more pertinent.

Judd took advantage not only of the grandly austere landscape around Marfa, however, but also of its built environment. He gradually acquired a number of vacant buildings to house his own work and the work of artists he admired, including storefronts, three ranches, and Fort D. A. Russell, which had been shut down after World War II. Judd renovated them, always in ways that reflected the artist's stringent standards. And, he designed furniture. Donald Judd's acquisitions and his lifestyle catalyzed a real estate revival in Marfa that would spawn curiosity among fans and seekers aspiring to live similarly vigorous creative lives in the untamed, open setting. He has come to be revered not just as the patron saint of minimalist art—although Judd preferred the term "empiricist"—but also as a champion of minimalist interiors, architecture, and furniture. He imagined and lived a minimal desert lifestyle.

Many of the houses in this book, interestingly, predate Judd's arrival. The desert outpost town featured humble structures of necessarily straightforward architecture, which ironically made them good candidates for conversions that reflect a present-day version of modernism. Restricted palettes of materials, edited details, plainspoken geometries, meticulously considered proportions, and a deliberate deference to the way light and shadow figure into the interiors fit perfectly with the often-harsh environment. In today's Marfa, these factors are amplified in unconventional ways, in part because of the difficulty in building in such a remote area. Homeowners and designers have to be inventive, so it's fortunate that the standard in Marfa is to be inclusive rather than exclusive. It's common, for instance, to find that the houses there were constructed with local materials and the assistance of local artisans. Or by the homeowners themselves. The result is an autonomous kind of modernism that's specific to Marfa and that also anticipated Judd's influence.

The goal for this volume was to include examples of the many kinds of modern that exist in Marfa. They fall generally into three broad categories. The first is vernacular modern, meaning old, probably adobe, and possibly historically significant structures that included elements of modernism out of necessity before the architectural movement existed. Next is handmade modern, or structures that are more ad hoc but express the simple volumes now identified with modernism. The last is recent modern, which refers to architect- or designer-conceived buildings.

Finding the houses to shoot was a major and of course crucial undertaking. My starting point was people I had written about as a writer and producer for *Metropolitan Home* magazine during my fourteen-year tenure there. My Rolodex from those days was invaluable. It was while shooting Tom and Suzanne Dungan's chic metal house in Houston, for example, that I first learned about the exodus from Houston to Marfa that was just beginning back in the 1990s. Marlys Tokerud is another Houstonian whose work I knew well. Both Suzanne and Marlys generously connected me with friends and colleagues who also had houses in or near Marfa that would fit our mission. Marfa's appeal of course stems from its remoteness and isolation, so discovering interesting properties was like unraveling a tightly wound ball of string. Conversations with Jamey and Constance Garza, Barbara Hill, Larry Doll, Jim Martinez, Kristen Bonkemeyer, Linda and Don Shafer, Lindsey and Ford Smith, Julie Speed and Fran Christina, Liz Lambert, Terry Nowell, and Jean Landry connected Casey Dunn and me to artisans and homeowners who generously contributed their homes, gardens, and art to our venture. We certainly felt lucky to be invited into these special properties. We are immensely grateful to the twenty-one homeowners who welcomed us.

It took us two years to shoot the houses in this book. We'd go out to Marfa for a week and shoot five houses at a time. I was the de facto stylist as well as author—my responsibility was to work with Casey to compose each shot, not only to be visually balanced, but to be sure we captured the homeowners' stylistic intentions. Normally I would bring lots of props to a shoot, but Casey and I agreed that the houses should be shot as straightforwardly as possible, with nothing extra added that wasn't already somewhere in the house. The usual flowers and edibles were also not appropriate, we decided—unless they were already there.

I discovered when I interviewed the homeowners for this book that many of them credited the grand landscape as the single most important reason for moving to Marfa, so we expected it to follow that all the houses would focus on a sweeping, dramatic scene. While many do, that didn't turn out to be everyone's reality—or intent. In some cases, the reason is simply economics: those views are expensive. But in other cases, people found themselves drawn to houses or former industrial buildings in the middle of town. Oddly, in a way it doesn't matter—the stunning views in Marfa are plentiful anyway and sometimes have nothing at all to do with the horizon line or mountain range. Some of the houses, such as Jean Landry and Richard Bullock's city house, look directly onto neighboring dwellings. A recently added, fenced courtyard off the couple's bedroom framed the sky in a new way for them, and that was enough; the sky in Marfa is justifiably famous in its own right, so now the couple has a prized view. The spectacle of changing clouds and light that gives way each night to innumerable stars is entertainingly varied. Other residences—such as chef Terry Nowell's handmade house—exude an interior richness; for him, the austere landscape serves as an antidote to the sensuality of the décor.

Many of the pleasures of Marfa are indeed visual, which explains why one of our greatest visual artists settled here and why others, such as Julie Speed and Michael Phelan, have followed. I would also affirm that every homeowner represented here deserves to be considered a visual artist in his or her own right. These thoughtful creatives carry on the tradition of Marfa as Donald Judd saw it: as a place where the demand to live for art is so compelling as to be unavoidable. In their own way, the houses presented here all are site-specific constructions that fulfill the spirit of Judd's command to make art suit its place.

—H. T.

Mystic   Cinder   Block

Jamey Garza and his wife, textile designer and former fashion designer Constance Holt-Garza, arrived in Marfa from Los Angeles in 2003 to work on the renovation of Liz Lambert's Thunderbird Hotel, having been called in after an earlier successful collaboration on Lambert's iconic Hotel San José in Austin in 1998. The couple thought they'd stay for a year and then move to Austin, Garza's hometown. More than a decade later, though, they're still living and working in Marfa, and operating their flourishing home-design company, Garza Marfa. He is a natural multitasker, though, so when he and Constance aren't working on their own residence—just across the street from their atelier—he helps design and build residences for clients all around town.

Such was the case in 2004 when he was approached by a unique Los Angeles–based couple looking to make a design connection in Marfa. They had purchased a lot on a highway a few blocks west of downtown, next to a little gas station, and were considering developing it into an event venue, perhaps a bar with live music. The spot was a logical location for an intimate roadhouse. "Reality set in, though," says Garza. "So did the logistics of going back and forth between Los Angeles and Marfa." Jamey helped the couple to revise the design to turn it into a private getaway instead, while keeping many of the elements intended for the roadhouse, such as the concrete floors. "Some of the basic footprint of the building stemmed out of that initial idea," he says.

"It helped determine where the walls went and where the kitchen and bath were to go."

The result is a 1,200-square-foot cinder-block house covered in gray stucco. A long screen porch on the west side protects the main entrance from the desert sun. The house and yard, landscaped by Austin-based Mark Word Design, are both enclosed by an 8-foot-high adobe wall that provides a physical as well as psychological barrier to the highway, which might be classified as a casually busy street in a bigger town. Garza used the golden ratio to establish the proportions of the 25-by-44-foot great room, which includes dining and sleeping areas. Exposed steel trusses frame cypress ceilings and add drama to the white hard-plaster walls. There's also a sleeping loft, attainable via stairs set into the wall by the doors to the screened porch. Behind and to one side of the fireplace is a bathroom; on the other lies a kitchen. "Relaxing, sleeping, and eating in one room makes sense in Marfa," he says, noting Donald Judd's influence. "He had beds everywhere."

The structure's most gaze-drawing features are unquestionably the steel-gridded, eight-pane clerestory windows that wrap three sides of the room. Boldly graphic inside and out courtesy of a rich orange hue of auto body lacquer, the high casement windows let in Marfa's celestial light and direct views upward and out—past the industrial setting outside and into the ever-changing desert sky.

This space morphed from intended event
venue into a private home, retaining some of
the elements along the way—such as concrete
floors—that make it hardy. A cypress ceiling
and steel trusses cover the main room, which
includes living, dining, sleeping, and cooking
spaces. The orange clerestory windows are
painted in auto body lacquer.

Hard white plaster walls inside this 1,200-square-foot house make a luminous contrast to the velvety gray stucco that covers the exterior of the cinder-block facade, overleaf. A screened porch on the west side offers both protection from the sun and a destination for perfect breeze-catching.

The

Box

Box

Architect Ron Rael refers to Marfa as a place of duality, where light and shade, old and new, rough and smooth, and industrial and handmade all share equal importance. Now a professor at the University of California, Berkeley, Rael was living in Marfa when a client sought his help designing a house that he could construct himself. Rael's professional focus is on the technology of craft and how it can be incorporated into site-specific structures, so the idea of a hand-built house was appealing to him and Virginia San Fratello, his partner in the Oakland-based firm Rael San Fratello.

"My client asked for a house that was modern and reflected the landscape," says Rael. Besides referencing traditional building practices, the client also wanted the house to acknowledge Donald Judd's contribution to the area, so they dubbed it The Box Box House. Rael and San Fratello's long rectangular template for the 1,200-square-foot dwelling features an interior, free-standing "box" that contains the most functional spaces—kitchen, bathroom, storage, and boiler. The main entry, which faces north, is a slice in the facade. That orientation serves the practical purpose of protecting it somewhat from the elements but also lends it a mysterious air since it's counterintuitively on the side of the house farthest from the street. At the other end, facing the street, a walled courtyard serves as an extension of the living room, accessible via a wall of glass doors.

The courtyard—which is protected on three sides by twelve-foot-high walls—is another reference to boxes. It elaborates on the theme of light and dark, its sun-filled space an antidote to the cool interiors. It also connects the house to the sky directly via the living area.

"People look at this house from the exterior and think it doesn't have windows," says Rael. The glass wall into the courtyard serves as one, however, and on the east facade, a broad, concrete-linteled portal opens onto a patio set with a concrete-and-steel fireplace, its boxy shape another homage to Judd. In the bedroom, a window butts against the north wall and gently guides the morning light into the room. A sense of tranquility is fostered by twenty-inch-thick earthen walls, a swirl of mud and brick that's plastered with local soils mixed with cactus mucilage, horse manure, and straw on both the interior and exterior. The owner takes a certain pleasure in the earthy interaction required to maintain a mud house. "You have to resurface it," he says about the dynamic nature of the building material. After he purchased the house he engaged San Fratello to complete the landscape design; the plan introduces an organized system of ocotillo, mesquite, yucca, and sotol close to the house that disperses to merge into wildness farther from the building. Jamey Garza of Garza Marfa also contributed to later design changes, such as fitting out the patio and fireplace.

The linear simplicity of contemporary furniture, such as the living room's cot and pillows, which were designed by Jamey Garza, previous pages, a B&B Italia sofa, left, and the Bertoia chairs at the dining table, above, contrast intriguingly with the residence's complexly rustic building material—a mix of local soil, cactus mucilage, horse manure, and straw. The colorful mobile in the dining area is by Toshi, and the ink-and-paper piece above the sofa is by local artist Laszlo Thorsen-Nagel, who originally hails from Bavaria.

A courtyard surrounded by high, rammed-earth walls buffers these large living room windows from the street and also functions as a private sculpture garden. Industrial elements act as a foil to the natural materials that give the house soul, including concrete floors that help to reflect light throughout the interior, and steel windows and doors that endow the building with modernity and structure.

Views to the landscape are carefully framed. Some emphasize the far-off horizon, others invite a focused look at nearby plantings. The bedroom window, right, is placed to assure that the direct morning light is the first thing the owners experience.

Handmade   Heartfelt

Terry Nowell's deceptively modest dwelling on a quiet side street is an artisanal riff on site-specific modernism, inspired by Donald Judd's insistence on the role of place in art. Nowell, an Austin-based chef, was on his way to Big Bend in the early 1990s when he made a detour to look at a house in Marfa that some friends were considering buying. The house had been tied up in legal limbo, though, since the homeowner had died intestate. Not only that, it had been abandoned for thirty-eight years, had no running water, and electricity came courtesy of the antiquated knob-and-tube wiring so common in the United States between the 1880s and the 1930s. And there was no deed. The friends eventually decided not to pursue the complicated project, but Nowell was instantly smitten. After four years of putting aright five different people's claims to the house, Nowell purchased it in 1995.

The adobe structure on a double lot was originally a one-room house with an outdoor horno kitchen. The first homeowner and his brothers added three additional rooms, including an indoor kitchen and bathroom, around 1957. Later, Nowell began remodeling his new purchase. That took him another eight years. The folk art collector called it slow going. "I never had the funds to just dial up a builder and say 'have at it,'" Nowell recalls. So he did it all himself.

With the help of architect and friend Bob Zetnick and construction advice from builder and friend Billy Marginot, Nowell updated the infrastructure, raised the downstairs ceilings from seven feet to ten, added a bathroom, modernized the kitchen, and added an upstairs sleeping loft to the tiny house. It now totals a proud 800 square feet. The original building was made with adobe blocks, so he had new adobes shipped in from New Mexico. The exterior and interior scratch, brown, and finish coating is Portland cement over the natural adobe block—not natural earthen plaster, the usual choice for a house of this vintage—which the multitasker chose for its durability. As a reminder of provenance, the chef left an unplastered "truth window" in the downstairs bedroom that exposes the original, thick adobe blocks that weigh around forty-five pounds each.

Nowell also made the outdoor benches, outdoor bathtub, wardrobes, desk, dining table, concrete sink, bed platforms, various side tables, art pedestals, concrete countertops, and cabinetry. "Now that all the hard work is done, I can say there is something very satisfying about sleeping in the beds I built, hanging clothes in furniture I built, and sitting in a room I decorated," he says about his handmade house that's in itself a work of art.

This house reveals the owner's hand in many
ways. Terry Nowell painted the portrait that
hangs above the sofa in the living room as well
as the red ladder he built that leads to a sleeping
loft he constructed, for example.

In the dining room, left, Nowell's sturdy, hand-built, dried-pecan-and-Honduran-mahogany dining table waits for additional guests to join four Odd Fellows hand-painted screen masks and a figurative painting by Steven Hull. The wood truck, above, is by Earl Simmons; atop it is a Sad Ghost by Marcel Dzama. Nowell built the wood side table.

Nowell propped a desiccated *Agave parryi* stalk from his yard into a
corner of the downstairs bedroom to emphasize the ceiling height.
A "truth window" above the pair of windows exposes the original
adobe brick. Nowell also made the white pine bed, the wood block
table, the desk, and the floor lamp. A pair of mud paintings by
Jimmy Lee Sudduth rests above the headboard, and the painting
above the desk is by the Rev. George P. Kornegay. Nowell paired a
chair from the Marfa Masonic Lodge with an English school chair
to frame the door into the dining room, right.

Even shower plumbing makes a sculptural statement thanks to Nowell's ingenuity; he expanded the bathroom's boundary by adding an enclosed courtyard and a hand-built hot tub. A birdhouse stands by—an option to nesting in the resident fir tree.

Filling

Station

Contemporary

The contemporary American landscape is an object of special fascination for New York–based conceptual artist Michael Phelan. In 2006, Ballroom Marfa commissioned an outdoor installation from the native Texan for the organization's courtyard. While working on it, he noticed a mauve-colored, abandoned filling station across the highway—a "For Sale" sign hung in front. "I had never been there before," Phelan says, "and I wasn't looking for a home." Despite those disclaimers, Phelan arranged a viewing of the property and immediately afterward told the realtor, "I'll take it."

The building was originally a Texaco service station and bus stop, and later became Colomo Handy Store. At 4,000 square feet, it had all the basic elements needed for a loftlike space, something Phelan was familiar with after having lived for years in New York. "It was a blank slate," he says. The concrete floor had stains on it leftover from car battery acid—the student of American culture not only liked the look, he kept it when he renovated the building. Inside, he painted the cinder-block walls white; the exterior got a coat of black. "That's my New York sensibility," he says.

The front room—obviously the place where sales were conducted—is now a game room complete with a tournament-worthy table-tennis table and parking spaces for two Cruiser bicycles. Phelan's living room, formerly the functioning garage, still has the original concrete floors and twelve-foot-high wood ceilings supported by steel beams. Phelan's locally made twenty-foot-long dining table occupies one side of the 1,000-square-foot room, but daybeds and lounge chairs suggest plenty of seating options for guests. Big walls offer the right backdrop for Phelan's big art.

Two bedrooms and two baths have also been carved out of the space and are connected to the main living area by a galley kitchen. Outdoor dining lies just beyond the eight-foot-tall wood-and-steel doors, in an enclosed back courtyard. Despite the interior hominess, the exterior still retains its mien of service, although now the forecourt where the pumps once stood has more of a porte cochere sensibility. Embedded deep in the attitude of the iconic structure is a commercial lure; something still beckons people to drive up and get out of their cars. "People stop in all the time," says Phelan. "They think this is something else to see, and they just walk in." The artist doesn't mind—it's a part of the American cultural landscape and the Marfa experience. "I have always had a certain odd desire to live in a gas station," Phelan says.

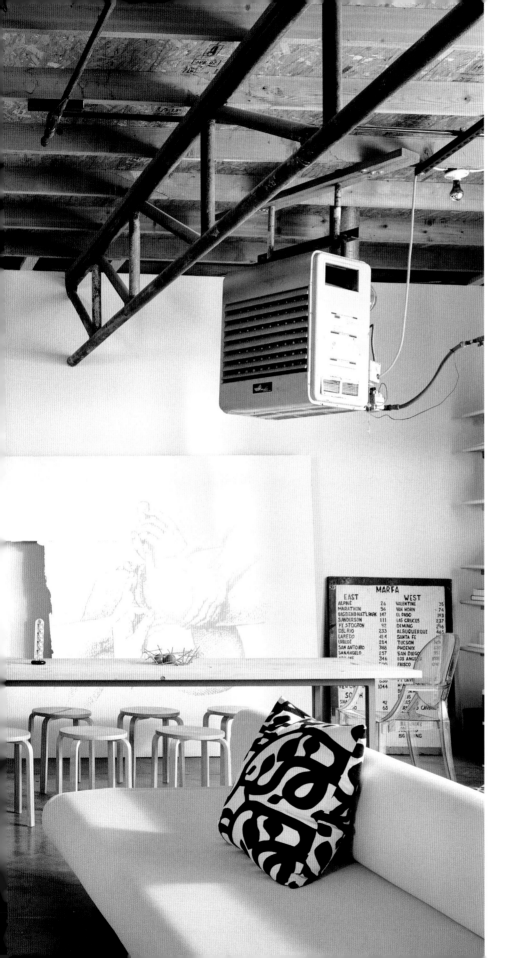

Michael Phelan left the original steel trusses and rafters exposed, previous pages and left, in this former gas station to help define space in the capacious commercial building. White-painted original cinder-block walls provide vast areas for a display of his own art as well as pieces by his favorite artists. The scored concrete floors are also original to the building.

A plywood ceiling in the bedroom, left, subdues the high ceiling and adds a natural wood-grain pattern overhead. Phelan painted provocative questions on one exterior wall, above, tantalizing passing drivers to slow to a stop at the intersection in front of his residence.

The automobile made a true impact on the commercial Marfa of old, since it was one of the few places to get a car serviced in this remote part of the state. The Inde/Jacobs Gallery was originally located in the sheet metal remains of a crumbling old Volkswagen repair shop known as George's Garage. Vilis Inde and Tom Jacobs eventually purchased the two lots where George's stood with the intention of building a new gallery on the site.

Inde was practicing law in New York in the late 1980s when he began building an art collection, a passion that became so consuming that he quit the legal world and decided to open an art gallery. After visiting Marfa with his partner, Tom Jacobs, the pair noticed that although a few galleries in town specialized in minimalist art, none exhibited art by the minimalist masters Donald Judd and Dan Flavin themselves, or by other artists associated with Chinati. By chance Marten Claesson, Eero Koivisto, Deta Koivisto Gemzell, and Ola Rune visited their early gallery. They are the principals in a multidisciplinary industrial design and architecture office based in Stockholm known for embracing New Millennium aesthetics. The group had an instant rapport, so plans were made for the architects to design a new gallery—that would also include a residence.

Plays on perspective inform the final structure. It's positioned perpendicular to the street on its rather mundane two lots so as to take advantage of the entire width of the property to powerful effect. It's actually two buildings—a gallery and a residence connected by long facade walls but separated by a shared courtyard. The exterior wall defining the yard runs the length of the lot and is a little off-angle, which creates an optical illusion giving the impression that the space alongside the house is even longer than it is.

The gallery is one big space, though punctuated by unique interior walls, a skylight, and a storage space. Walls around the skylight don't touch the floor, and the walls around the storage space don't touch the ceiling—this creates an equalizing balance of vertical dynamics in the room. The courtyard between the gallery and the house serves both as a garden for the house and a sculpture garden for the gallery. It also expands the livable space for the compact residence, which consists of a living room that opens onto the courtyard and a galley kitchen and master suite at the back of the building, farthest from the street.

This is a house built for living, but also for art. The architects were firm in their conviction about how a gallery space should function: "A room for art should either heighten the experience of the art displayed in it or it shouldn't make itself present at all," Ola Rune comments in their book about the project, *Claesson Koivisto Rune in Marfa*. The all-white residence and gallery are designed to help it recede in an unobtrusive way—both from the perspective of the viewer in the street as well as from a visitor stepping inside. Its evanescent color and structure is both there and not there, heightening the sense that the art is all that needs to be seen.

Pard Morrison's fired-pigment-on-aluminum
sculpture *Schneewittchen*, 2013, stands tall
in a courtyard between the gallery side of the
building and the residence. An orange chair by
Donald Judd is just visible beyond, in the gallery.

Box shapes play a dominant role in the gallery's design, where two cubes—one elevated, the other grounded—provide walls for art display. The architects, Claesson Koivisto Rune, also designed a small collection of accessories they dubbed the Marfa Collection for the space; their Marfa Mezzanine coffee table sits between the sofas in the gallery and is large enough for reviewing art prints. Its materials, angles, and proportions relate directly to the building's features.

Squares appear as a recurring motif throughout
the bedroom, above and left, as with the
bookshelves, the chair, the blanket across
the foot of the bed, and the windows.

A grid pattern inlaid in the interior courtyard defines the space in relation to the vertical expansion joints in the building's stucco facade, left. The seemingly regular shape is intentionally, subtly skewed in the exterior courtyard that stretches the length of the two buildings: the architects play with visitors' perspectives by setting the freestanding wall at a slight angle to make the space seem longer when viewed from the street.

Art in Place

The one-and-a-third–acre property that belongs to painter Julie Speed and her husband, musician Fran Christina, would be a dream for any Donald Judd fan: the L-shaped compound of buildings abuts Fort D. A. Russell, where Judd placed his fifteen untitled concrete works in a field. The land looks like it should be part of the fort—and, indeed, it was. The jail was located there, but after World War II it was purchased by the Texas Land Bank Credit Union and became a bank; the rest of the lot was paved over. Despite its institutional ambience, every time Speed and Christina visited Marfa, the artist would comment on how much she would love to buy the property. The land was eventually put up for sale and offered to the Chinati Foundation; when they turned it down, the couple snapped it up.

"The original idea was to turn the jail into our house," says Christina. He started a two-year process of demolishing the interior of the building, but it soon became apparent that too many compromises to the aesthetics of the bunker-like concrete building would be required to turn it into a dwelling. They finally had to admit it wasn't truly the home of their dreams anyway. However, because Speed is an artist who shifts constantly between oil painting, drawing, printmaking, collage, and gouache, the layout of the jail's many long rooms suited her artistic practice perfectly. The jail became her studio, and provides separate workspaces for separate mediums, plus an office, art storage, and Christina's studio, where he produces limited editions of his wife's etchings.

So the couple decided to build a new house. Speed regularly carries a tape measure in order to record proportions of things that please her, and on the occasions when she forgets it, her husband's feet come in handy since they are exactly one foot long. The artist discovered, after measuring room after room, that she was always most comfortable inside a double square—where the length is exactly double the width. The double square became the standard for the rooms in the new house, particularly the living room, which is sized as two double squares.

Speed and Christina designed and built the house themselves, so they were able to match all the curves of the retaining walls, the arch under the outside stairway, and even the curve of a birdbath foundation to the curve of the roofs of the artillery sheds that house Judd's works in aluminum. The multitasking couple created precisely what they needed to pursue their various interests. One of his is music—he was the drummer for the blues rock band The Fabulous Thunderbirds for twenty-one years. The couple carefully sited the house and its second-story sunporch so that those concrete pieces would be within constant view.

The final 2,200-square-foot house is constructed with Hebel block—autoclaved, aerated concrete—and is built to last. The main structure contains the living space/kitchen, and a smaller attached structure contains the master suite. It also includes a pantry, stairs up to a low-ceilinged guest loft, and stairs down to a basement. All rooms open to the porch and the view along the back.

The compound is a work in progress. The couple continues to embellish, add on, fix up, and refine the structures that help them to work and to live fulfilling lives. As an active element of the couple's creative processes, the dwellings do more than merely contain Speed and Christina's art—they have become art in their own right; art that happens to be nicely aligned in proportion with the inspiring and ever-present concrete boxes by Donald Judd.

Numerous long rooms in the former jail allow Speed to set up separate studio spaces for oil and paper, previous pages, as well as an office and art storage. In the new house that she and husband Fran Cristina built, left, Speed uses wall space as an ever-changing venue for a display of her own paintings and favorites by other artists.

In the dining area, left, a replica of the battleship Potemkin by Speed's father is on display in a glass case; mismatched chairs provide seating at a table Cristina fashioned from a veterinarian's examination table and reclaimed oak. Chinese-inspired stoneware and porcelain pottery crowned with tiny teapots are the handiwork of Julie Speed's mother and receive pride of place in the kitchen, above, near ginger jars filled with birdseed.

The walls in the master bedroom, above, are
painted a luminous light gray. The floors are
rift-and-quarter-sawn oak planks; they extend
throughout the main house. Judd's works in
concrete are always on view from the couple's
second-story sunporch.

Outside

the

Box

San Antonio–based architecture firm Lake|Flato is known for designing modern residences that tell a backstory about Texas's agricultural past. The firm advocates including vernacular elements such as big overhangs, trellises, courtyards, outdoor showers, and porches, and these have now become the building blocks of a line of prefab houses the firm calls Porch Houses.

Each house is basically the shape of a shipping container, although Lake|Flato offers a choice of lengths. They are factory-built in a range of materials seventy miles outside of Houston, transported to the final site, and then adapted to the terrain. Leftover materials are recycled. The Porch House is another way Ted Flato and David Lake have continued to promote the romance of the Texas terrain—accessing the surrounding landscape is meant to be effortless and pleasurable, via a wall of sliding-glass doors and through doors at either end of the building. "We like to make people go outside," says Bill Aylor, an associate partner. "Whether they are taking a shower, drinking a beer, or—even better—doing both."

In 2013, Aylor was contacted by two artists who were looking for a way to build a house on a remote, off-the-grid site where they would have a feeling of isolation and could venture out to experience nature.

The property was deep into the topography just north of Fort Davis—through two ranches and up the steep and rocky face of a mountain. "The last six miles require a four-wheel-drive vehicle for access," says Aylor, "and in extreme weather you can't get in or out." The couple purchased two Porch House modules—a 40-foot-long living unit and a 17-foot-long bedroom unit—and Aylor placed them in a line with a dogtrot between. A 140-foot-long sheet of Galvalume functions as one long, gabled roof that covers the three spaces and terminates in a carport. "We wanted to keep it simple," he says, "because the scale of the landscape is so big." The house is indeed perched above a canyon, which makes it feel somewhat like a ship jutting out into open water; the owners have dubbed it "The Prow."

The clients use the two-bedroom, two-bath, 1,326-square-foot house summer and winter, and depend on a 19,000-gallon rainwater collection tank to supply all their water. Air-conditioning is courtesy of open doors and windows, and heating comes from a very efficient fireplace and from supplemental heat — a photovoltaic array that includes solar panels and an integrated battery generates electricity.

Two Lake|Flato Porch House modules—one 40-foot-long living unit and one 17-foot-long bedroom unit—are connected by a dogtrot and capped with a 140-foot-long Galvalume roof. Access to the outdoors is effortless, via a wall of rolling perforated metal doors. An outdoor shower with a view to the grand terrain is part of the experience.

The unabashed use of pastels in this otherwise
rustic interior suggests a stylish disregard of the
concept of roughing it. The pink sofa, layered
carpets, and custom yellow cabinetry are civilizing
gestures in a dwelling that otherwise fosters a
sense of isolation from the outside world.

Doors and windows provide natural ventilation, but heat comes from a very efficient fireplace and a solar thermal system. Bamboo floors and pine walls also contribute to an overall feeling of general warmth.

Dance Hall

Minimal

Houston-based architectural designer Barbara Hill has always been a contrarian—she calls herself a minimalist at heart, but one with a vibrant understanding of luxury. The red-haired Miss Texas 1956 would prefer to remove decorative and architectural elements than to add them, and she stuck to that mantra while renovating this adobe building on a third of an acre a few blocks from downtown Marfa. The hundred-year-old structure, originally built as a private dance hall, has seen many incarnations, from a grocery and candy store to simply a derelict building. When Hill first saw it, it was a warren of rooms filled with trash. She spent a year and a half transforming it into a sophisticated desert retreat that has now become her home away from home.

First Hill cleaned the place out, filling eight dumpsters and many flatbed trailers with trash and construction scrap. In doing so, the designer realized that every single thing that made the place seem cramped could be removed. She became obsessed with returning the building to what it once had been—essentially one large room. In the process of digging out rotted floorboards, she discovered several pits underneath the building that suggested the building's adobe had been sourced on site. The discovery delighted the purist in Hill. She appreciates adobe for its insulating qualities, noise-muffling solidity, and the slight scent of earth it leaves in the air.

The trickiest part of the renovation involved stabilizing the walls to allow for a higher ceiling. Structural engineer Dan Ray proposed immense steel beams to shore up the tension—adobe can withstand enormous vertical pressure, but it will buckle from too much pressure on the sides. Although it was cost prohibitive to create high ceilings throughout, Hill opted for a soaring central space with birch plywood for flooring and as a liner for the pitched part of the ceiling. This is flanked by two areas with lower, ten-foot ceilings in the eating and sleeping zones. About her decision to place the bathtub in the middle of the bedroom, Hill simply says that it brings her joy to see it when she wakes up because she thinks it looks a little like a cowboy boot. For the modest, there's also a private bathroom and shower.

A courtyard anchored by a sculptural steel "campfire" designed by Houston- and Marfa-based artist George Sacaris leads to the entry to the residence, which is via an east-facing wall of steel-and-glass doors. Incorporating a welcoming outdoor area was important to Hill because she finds the light in Marfa lovely and likes to live outdoors whenever the weather permits. Both tourists and locals often poke their heads over the courtyard wall to admire the garden created by Marfa resident and landscape architect Jim Martinez. Hill doesn't mind. It's one of the things she loves about Marfa.

The house is located downtown and passersby, curious to see what's beyond the wall, often peer over the top for a look. Their curiosity is rewarded by a view of a fire pit by Houston- and Marfa-based metal artist George Sacaris that anchors the front yard.

Designer Barbara Hill used birch plywood
on both the ceiling and the floor, for visual
continuity. She employed a dropped ceiling
over the bedroom area of the vast loftlike space
for definition of function, as well as to establish
a more cozy environment for sleeping. Hill
favors strong design statements—she extended
the entire kitchen across one wall, overleaf,
and emphasized the gesture with an extra-wide
industrial sink. The Poetry chairs at right are
custom made by Hill, with pithy excerpts from
romance novels inscribed on the upholstery.

Bathtubs function as sculpture to the designer,
as is evident from this exposed tub placed in the
middle of the bedroom space and in plain sight
of the living area.

White plaster walls add luminous glamour to the rough-and-ready décor, such as a second industrial sink and a formerly illuminated metal sign that's now sans lights. Deep-set windows throughout soften Marfa's glaring midday light and suggest that the hefty structure is here to stay.

Private

Compound

The high desert butts up to the foothills of the Davis Mountains in Fort Davis, twenty-one miles north of Marfa. The horizon isn't long and low like it is in Marfa, rather it is dominated by the bulky igneous prows of the mountains. It's not hard to see that the uplifted intrusions are the remains of magma spewed up by volcanoes sixty-five million years ago. Mount Locke towers at 6,790 feet and is where McDonald Observatory was established in 1933. These scenic features drew Anne Adams when she decided to retire from her job as the registrar at The Menil Collection in Houston. Her father had served on the board of visitors of the observatory so Adams made the trek from the family's Fort Worth home to Fort Davis frequently when she was a child.

Adams sought the help of a friend, Houston-based decorator Marlys Tokerud, also a part-time resident of Marfa, to help her envision her new home. She hired Kristin Bonkemeyer, a Marfa-based architect, to design it. Some elements were essential to Adams: "I wanted the feel of a compound, and I wanted privacy." She also wanted her house to be clad in corrugated metal, since the material is hardy, heat resistant, and economical. Bonkemeyer's familiarity with the desert landscape expresses itself in the way she sited Adams's house.

The concrete, Hardie cement board, and Galvalume building stretches parallel to nearby rugged mountain cliffs with a two-bedroom guest suite on one end, the living area in the middle, and the master suite at the other end. Two porches embrace the 3,200-square-foot dwelling and account for half its footprint. "One is for the morning," says Adams, "and the other is for evening; at the last minute, we screened that one in."

Houstonians will recognize the color Adams chose for the house's facade—a soft Sherwin-Williams gray known fondly as "Doville Gray"—a nod to the color Dominique de Menil painted the single-story bungalows in the ten-block area around the museum where Adams worked for forty years. The color, paired with the modernist lines of the house, has a softening effect. "The sun is glaring here," says Adams, "and this soft gray makes a retreat from all that glare." Another antidote to the desert heat and brightness is the color Adams chose for her interior: a serene white that envelops the walls and pitched-plank living room ceiling with atmospheric calm. Adams populated her new residence with a few family antiques, then enlivened them with more modern pieces from Tokerud Interiors. "Out here," she says, "I wanted it to feel modern."

Architect Kristin Bonkemeyer and interior designer Marlys
Tokerud plotted with client and recent retiree Anne Adams to
infuse this corrugated metal house with references to the past
as well as acknowledgments of the future. The exterior of the
corrugated metal compound is painted the same shade of gray that
Houston arts patron Dominique de Menil painted the single-story
bungalows in the ten-block area around the museum where Adams
worked for forty years. Inside, cool white interiors are decorated
with a mix of modern furniture and Adams's heirlooms.

The master bedroom suite, above, is at one end of the compound; two guest rooms are at the other. Floors are concrete throughout, but Bonkemeyer softened the building's crisp modernity by including a wood-plank ceiling painted white.

Two porches—one for the morning and one for evening enjoyment—embrace the 3,200-square-foot dwelling and account for half of its square footage. Adams is an avid bird-watcher, so Bonkemeyer installed a kitchen window that looks into and through the screened "evening" porch for handy viewing at dusk.

Bunkhouse Modern

"This landscape is instilled in me," says native Odessan Liz Lambert about the land around Marfa where she now lives. "It feels like home here." And indeed, she has made a spiffed-up former bunkhouse her home. The adobe structure lies between Fort Davis and Marfa, and belongs to her uncle. The trendsetting hotelier has had plenty of experience with creating design-infused homes away from home—in the late 1990s, with the help of Lake|Flato Architects, Lambert turned a seedy motel on Austin's South Congress Avenue into the hippest hotel in town; doing so inspired a citywide tourism renaissance that is still going strong. The Hotel San José was the beginning of a turnaround for a part of Austin that is now the firmly entrenched favorite of scenesters. Ten years later, she adapted the idea for Marfa, renovating the 1950s-era Thunderbird Hotel into a boutique hotel complete with a pool in the courtyard that is quite literally an oasis in the desert. In 2006, she turned a large plot of land in Marfa into El Cosmico, a "nomadic hotel and campground" filled with Spartan trailers, tepees, tents, yurts, and wood-fired hot tubs.

Although Lambert has other options, this boxy 1930s-era bunkhouse with its unintentionally modernist silhouette is where she comes to get away from it all. Lambert has enlivened the utilitarian interior with colorful art and eclectic, found furnishings. "I made it up as I went along," she says. The ad hoc revival included turning a laundry room to the right of the living/dining room into her bedroom, adding a second bath, and emboldening the kitchen with Moroccan-style tiles and a big stove underneath a bank of windows. A screened-in porch just beyond the kitchen shelters a long table where Lambert's many parties spill. It's a house set up for good times, and to accommodate guests and necessities Lambert has added a row of miniature outbuildings in back, one for laundry and another for bathing. A pleasant option is to open the small structure fully to the elements by opening the doors and windows, to catch breezes and a close-up view of the mountain rising immediately behind. "Everything goes away when I am out here," says Lambert. "This is a good place to come and think things over."

Hotelier Liz Lambert enlivened the interior of this 1930s-era former bunkhouse where she goes to get away by making things up as she went along. One move was to add contemporary chairs to a porch that boasts views toward both Marfa and Fort Davis; another was to mix and match colorful chairs on the simply refinished interior.

The house's ad hoc revival includes clever uses of industrial materials. Part of a vintage metal sign makes a fine sliding door that closes off the kitchen from the dining area, for example, and a "chandelier" fashioned from a long piece of pipe serves well to light the dinner table at night. Lambert also fortified the simple kitchen, overleaf, with Moroccan-style tiles. A screened-in porch just beyond the kitchen shelters a long table made of industrial drums and a plank.

A water tank, above, is a short jeep ride from the house—it's a favorite spot for a quick swim and some respite on the deck while admiring the view. Lambert has added a row of modernist-inspired outbuildings behind the house as well, one of which is for laundry and another, right, for bathing while contemplating a craggy mountain up close.

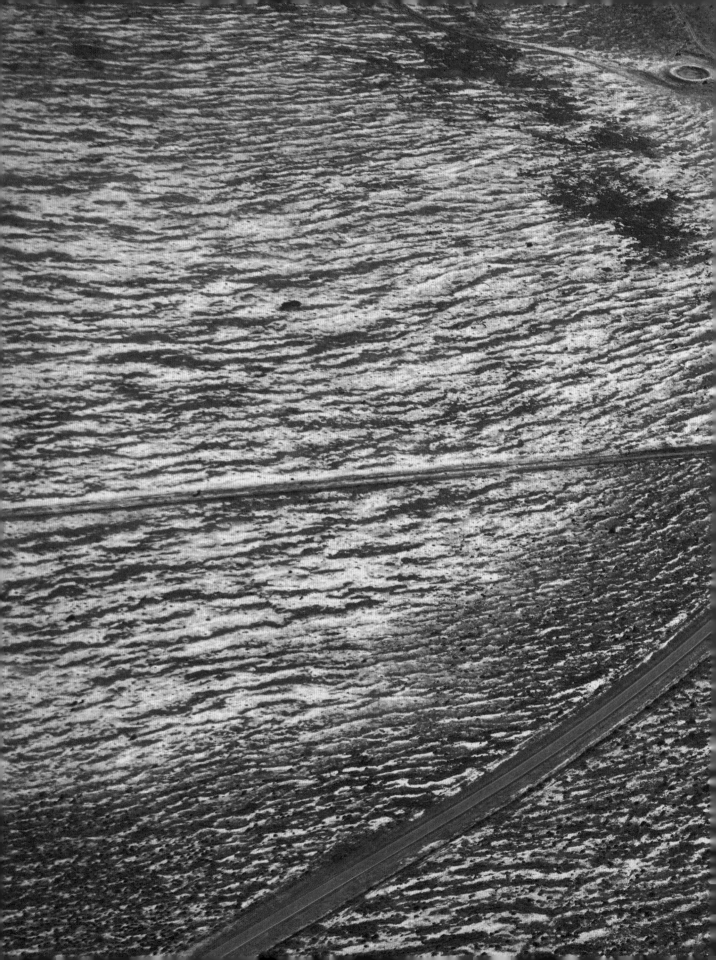

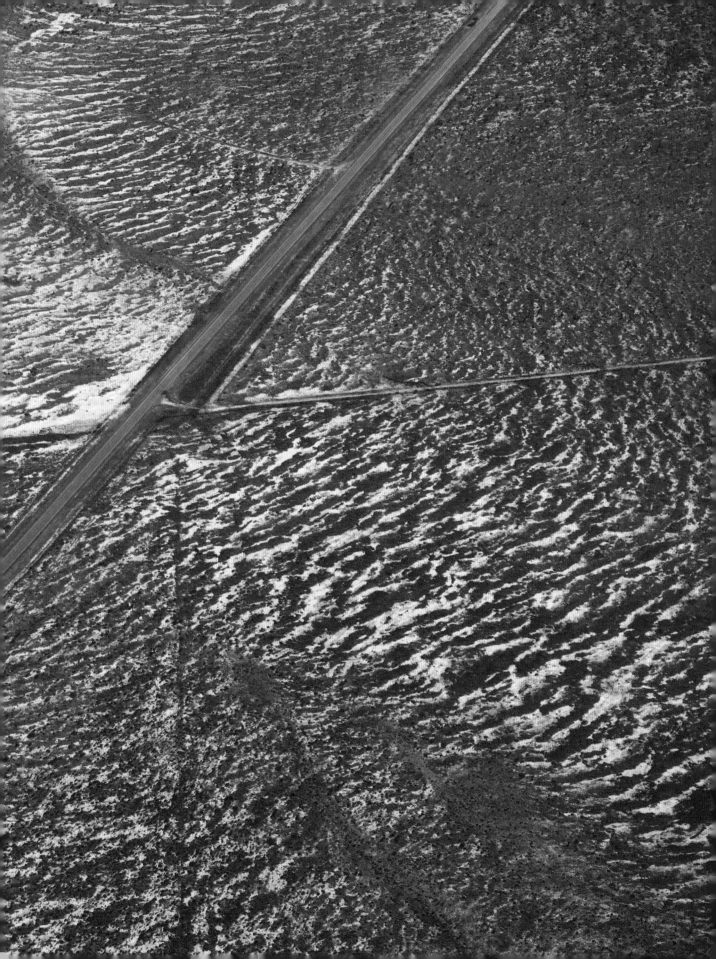

Material   Aesthetic

Larry and Laura Doll live across the country from each other—she in San Francisco, where she is a regulatory relations executive with Pacific Gas & Electric, and he in Austin, where he is an associate professor of architecture and the founding director of the European study abroad program at the University of Texas at Austin. The first time Larry visited Marfa was with his students in 1991, but that Christmas he returned with Laura and after that a seasonal trip to West Texas became a tradition for the couple. They had stayed in various locations—Marathon, Lajitas, Fort Davis, and Marfa—but in 1998 Laura commented to her husband that they kept returning to Marfa and should probably look for a house there to renovate. "We looked around for an hour," says Larry, "and couldn't find anything."

Instant gratification was at hand, though; they happened to pass a "For Sale" sign on some midslope lots on a hill that looked toward the Davis Mountains. The lots were 42 by 100 feet each, "proportioned almost as if they were designed for a trailer," says Larry. They immediately bought two, then once Larry had designed a house, they bought two more to secure the view from their bedroom window. "My first idea was to do rammed earth," the architect says. Finding artisans and contractors who were conversant with the damp mixture of earth, sand, gravel, and clay proved to be difficult, so the Dolls opted for adobe bricks instead. "You have to accept the limitations of the materials and the skill sets in any area," says Larry. "Adobe is well suited for the Marfa climate and culture."

The couple began discussions with Steve Belardo of Rainbow Adobe in Alpine. "He had a long waiting list," says Larry, "which was fine, because I had to go through

a couple designs to get the one we liked." They decided on a long, rectangular building with one bedroom and two and a half baths, plus an accompanying casita with a living zone and a sleeping zone separated by one of the baths. Larry was pragmatic about the design he came up with: "I wasn't going to be around for a lot of the construction process, so I created something where mistakes would be acceptable." That's another way of saying that the design was driven by the materials at hand. "I treated them as an aesthetic condition," he says. The bricks were made on site with adobe stabilized with an 11-percent mix of Portland cement. "That was the reason we didn't have to plaster the exterior," says Larry about the decision. "The trick with an adobe structure," he says, "is that it has to have a bond beam around the upper perimeter—a cap that the roof actually sits on. Adobe has no tensile strength," he says. "The bottom just sits on the ground."

The adobe bricks used for the house became an aesthetic statement inside and out, the repeated rectangular shapes echoing the shape of the residence, its casita, and the four lots that preserve the view to the mountains. Because the brick pattern is so assertive, decorative flourishes are unnecessary for the minimal-minded buildings. Larry deliberately left the space between the buildings open, without a wall. "I like the way the prairie comes between them," he notes. Both buildings have porches positioned to take in the scenery, a pastime that is one of the main reasons the busy couple keeps making time for Marfa. "Its remoteness and natural splendor are antidotes to stress and make us feel like we have gotten away from everything."

The windows were welded on site, and with
an intentionally small profile; Doll wanted to
emphasize their contrast to the monolithic walls
and to juxtapose smooth and rough planes. He
left the deep reveals exposed inside and placed
the bottom of the windows at floor level so that
light would bounce off the waxed concrete floors.

Doorways and windows are aligned in an enfilade so that views to the landscape can be enjoyed through the length of the house. Doll arranged for certain views, however, to be appreciated from outside the house: "That's what the porch is for." It also offers a close-up look at the prairie, which Doll and landscape architect Jim Martinez invited to grow between the main house and the casita.

There is a reason that a nondescript box of a house is usually a good candidate for a modernist renovation—once it's stripped of all the add-ons and other embellishments applied over the years, the only thing left is a pure shape. Squares and rectangles are enduring silhouettes firmly embedded in the canon of modernism, as well as in the gleaming minimalism embodied by Donald Judd's steel boxes. That's what attracted designer Barbara Hill to this tiny adobe house near downtown Marfa, a house that was, in fact, even smaller than she bargained for. "It sat so close to its neighbor," she says, "that I always thought it was one house."

"The plan was to clean it up and rent it," says Hill, who has renovated two other houses in Marfa. She purchased tiles and a sink to refresh the bathroom, which, of all the 864-square-foot house's four rooms, was ostensibly in the worst shape. "Then one thing led to another," she says. The two front rooms with eleven-foot ceilings—one a living room, the other a bedroom—were probably original, opined builder Billy Marginot, who also guesses they were constructed in the 1800s. A kitchen and bath occupied the middle of the house; another bedroom built out of cinder block had been tacked on in back and opened onto a sort of ad hoc back porch.

Hill likened this renovation process to an archaeological dig, and in this case her digging revealed some great finds. Her "design disease" kicked in when she removed the acoustical-tile ceiling in the two front rooms to discover that there were three additional feet above and that the original ceilings were clad in beadboard—which she of course wanted to preserve. "That set my heart racing," she says. "I was off and running." Next she removed the wood flooring that sat right on top of the dirt underneath, replacing it with concrete throughout the house. She completely gutted the kitchen, transformed the front bedroom into a dining room that opens onto the living room, and rebuilt the bath and bedroom. The designer also occupied the tiny house with a lively selection of midcentury furniture, vintage finds, and funky art.

Now the airy, light-filled house is a merry reminder that a century's worth of prescience preceded the modernist movement.

Hill installed pink neon behind a seven-foot-tall Elvis-as-gunslinger print, previous pages, that presides over the dining table and its two colors of Bertoia chairs. Other art in the great room, above, includes a piece by Claire Cusack above Gervasoni's Ghost sofa—the artist grouped windmill blades and arrows she made from carnival pointers for art with a West Texas message. The white faux bois coffee table is by George Sacaris. In the kitchen, right, bright yellow recycled plastic chairs from DWR fit with a tall, marble-topped table from Installation in Houston.

The bar cart in the kitchen, above, is from Kuhl-Linscomb in Houston. Hill furnished the bedroom, right, with a vintage chest of drawers and a bed from DWR. The tiny house is next door to another house the designer owns, so she used both color and landscape plantings to unite the two.

Off the Grid

An element of mystery surrounds this metal-canopied steel, concrete, and glass house—because it's in plain view of both everything and nothing. Owner Michael Barnard says you can see it from fifty miles away. The two-bedroom, three-bath, solar-powered home sits on a mountaintop on 242 acres near Chinati Hot Springs; the Rio Grande River defines the southern edge of the ranch. Barnard, a doctor and developer who lives in Fort Worth, acquired this 2,200-square-foot off-the-grid dwelling from a French couple who periodically flew in from France to build it. The couple drove to the far reaches of the Texas desert in a truck they stored in a warehouse they rented from Barnard in the city. The pair divorced before the house was completed and sold it to Barnard, who understands what he considers to be the legacy of the property.

The original French owners were intent on building their own desert retreat, and sourced the building materials in Fort Worth. It was their idea to adapt the simplest of sunshades—a twenty-foot-tall pole barn—to soar above the boxy residence and shield the nearly open-air house. Breezes whisk in one side and out another via sliding doors on at least three sides of each of the living spaces, handily providing plenty of cross-ventilation. Since the view is all-important, Barnard placed what he calls "the ugly stuff"—the garage and solar panels—down the hill and out of sight. That clears the way for sighting mule deer, elk, javelina, aoudad, bighorn sheep, and birds of prey. Barnard has considerably cut a patch out of the roof so he and his guests can view the stars at night.

"I call this house 'integrated desert style,'" says Barnard, who fully credits Donald Judd with bringing West Texas's high desert landscape to the attention of the world. This is a place where a direct relationship with the environment is impossible to avoid, where nearly every growing thing either pricks or stings, where the heat is extreme and the cold is bitter, and where beauty is laced with an element of the frightening. Barnard has completed the job of constructing a brave outpost for both enjoying nature at its most gentle and being awed by its occasional fearsomeness. The genial canopy is at its most necessary when the sun is shining full blast, of course, but perhaps is at its most thrilling during a rainstorm, when the sights and sounds can be outlandishly terrific.

The original, French owners of this metal, concrete, steel, and glass house were intent on building a solar-powered desert retreat. It was their idea to adapt the simplest of sunshades— a 20-foot-tall pole barn—to soar above the boxy residence and to shield the nearly open-air house from the heat. Cross-ventilation is handily achieved via sliding doors on at least three sides of each of the living spaces so that breezes can whisk in one side and out the other.

Mod

Squad

The view from the living room and balcony of Linda and Don Shafer's house may be the most unexpected in the area—it focuses on Marfa itself instead of on the highly touted mountainscape that stretches along the horizon to the side and back of their modern steel-and-glass house. Prominently perched on a rocky rise that's the highest point in town, the U-shaped courtyard compound wasn't remotely what the couple had originally intended to build as a desert pied-à-terre.

The Shafers have been visiting Big Bend regularly over the past twenty-five years, to hike and raft. The arid high desert is an environment the couple is partial to, having lived in Santa Fe in the late 1970s and 1980s. They then moved to Austin, where she was the director of the Software Quality Institute at the University of Texas. Don is a serial entrepreneur and currently the chief technology office for a software company. Inevitably, though, Marfa got to them. "We fell in love with the landscape," says Linda.

The couple rented a house for a year before deciding to buy a historic adobe, a landmark built in 1914 that was known for being lavishly decorated at Christmas. "We hired an architect to take it back to its original grandeur," Linda says about the stucco-and-fired-tile structure. Unfortunately, their efforts weren't rewarded with good news. A bad renovation in the 1950s had irreparably severed a supporting beam—the structure was deemed unsound by both the architect and an engineer.

"We needed another option," remembers Don, "but building costs here approach those in New York," says Don, "because everything has to be shipped in." It would be cheaper, the Shafers discovered, to move an entire prefab house to Marfa than to build anew. They approached another Austinite, architect Chris Krager, whose Ma Modular buildings presented a deft solution. The prefab modules—as the Shafers learned firsthand—arrive on site fully equipped with plumbing, electrical fixtures, and appliances.

The couple decided on the configuration they wanted —a guesthouse and main house set at a 90-degree angle to each other. The living room is formed of two units, "kind of like two double-wide trailers merged together," says Don. A steel band running down the center is the telltale connector. The guest house is a separate unit, as is the master bedroom wing.

To sidestep the type of structural issues that defeated the couple's original renovation plans, the builder sunk concrete piers forty feet deep to guarantee long-term stability. The view determined the siting. "We wanted a big deck off the living room that faced south, toward town," said Linda. That vista includes a ranch house to the right, the town's iconic courthouse and cityscape, and the stretch of horizon beyond. Anytime, day or night, the deck is their favorite outpost—big thunderstorms and lighting roll in from the south and the ever-changing clouds keep the pair fascinated. "That's Texas to us," says Linda.

Austin-based Ma Modular prefab buildings
helped this hilltop property materialize. They
arrive on site fully equipped with plumbing,
electrical fixtures, and appliances; importing
each element to Marfa separately would have
made this scale of project cost prohibitive.

The view—which includes Marfa's Second Empire-style courthouse and the elongated horizon beyond—determined the orientation of the units' large windows. In the living room, left, a painting by family friend Will Klemm sets a Western tone inside the modern dwellings.

The configuration of modular units forms a
perfect U shape, and creates a courtyard between
the main house and the guest house. The Shafers
furnished the space in a minimalist vein, opting
for modernist pieces and a few local finds, such
as the saddle leather chair by Garza Marfa, right.

Sky Island

Appearances, as we know, can be deceiving. This 2,300-square-foot house seems inscrutable from the street, and a passerby would never guess that the building's two wings, which open eighty degrees to take in the north view, are as much glass as wall. Local landscape designer Jim Martinez and his partner, Jim Fissel, planned this Marfa house for years. The pair had first come to Marfa in 1998 for a symposium on art and architecture at the Chinati Foundation that featured Frank Gehry, Claes Oldenburg, Coosje van Bruggen, and Jacques Herzog, and they couldn't stop thinking about the town where environment and art merged so dynamically. The landscape was alluring in part because Martinez hails from New Mexico, so he was used to being immersed in a similarly arid environment. "Rolling grassland is like home to me," says Martinez. He and Fissel love to hike, so Marfa's proximity to Big Bend and the Guadalupe Mountains made their decision to build a house on this sky island practically inevitable—a welcome counterpoint to their busy urban lives in Dallas.

The couple purchased property near the highest point in town in 2003. Next they contacted Houston architect Cameron Armstrong, who was designing another residence in Marfa for Houston clients at the same time—meaning materials for both houses could be purchased together. Armstrong is known for his imaginative strategies, so he supported Martinez and Fissel's desire to build part of the house themselves, as well as their intention to use recycled materials and to waste nothing in the process of building their energy-efficient home. They were successful and pragmatic about it, too: "We didn't have a dumpster out here," notes Martinez. "What little waste there was ended up in the foundation."

Martinez and Fissel embraced innovative building materials, and were the first in town to use Hebel block: autoclaved, aerated concrete blocks that are one-third the weight of traditional concrete blocks and that have a high insulation value. The blocks are filled with green, LEED-applicable materials and can be stuccoed over without first applying wire lathe, thus saving time and expense. They also added solar panels to generate electricity for the entire house. On a more basic level, the design of the massive tongue-in-groove front "door"— really a gate that opens from an exterior courtyard into the interior courtyard—can be positioned to direct cooling breezes straight inside, where they waft over the concrete terraces outside the private and guest wings of the house, which sit nearly perpendicular to it.

The interior courtyard separates the couple's living quarters—living room, dining area, kitchen, powder room, and master suite—from the two-room guest suite and bath. Martinez uses one of the rooms as an office; Fissel works in a nook just off the kitchen. A steel staircase adds sculptural drama in the courtyard and leads to an upstairs terrace that provides a panoramic view of the world around Marfa. It's also sometimes enjoyed by a family of foxes that Martinez sees departing just after dawn.

Jim Martinez set an 80-degree angle between
the two wings of this house as a tribute to his
grandmother; her Mora Valley, New Mexico,
home had the same floor plan and also faced
east. In the courtyard, above and right, a colorful
panel by sculptor and installation artist Margo
Sawyer brightens up the stair landing. Jim Fissel
designed the tongue-in-groove pivot door to the
house, and the dried-pine ceiling extends into
the main house. The stairs are by local welder
Bill Parrot.

In the living room, above and right, a series by
Agnes Martin adds texture and rhythm to the
white walls and is a thoughtful antidote to the
rural desert environment.

Martinez uses one of the rooms in the guest wing as an office. The chairs at the dining table were made as part of a Works Progress Administration project in the 1930s; the green hand-built chair belonged to Martinez's great-grandmother.

The master bedroom, left, can be closed off from the main living space by a rolling barn door. The view from the bed is directly into the backyard, which Martinez has populated with native plants from the Chihuahuan desert. The painting is by Marfa-based artist Martha Hughes.

The house is sited in a rather exposed area, but native grasses thrive in the arid conditions. Martinez has created an experimental garden of taller specimens in the backyard, which cluster around the house to shade and protect it.

The Power of Paint

When Houston interior designer Marlys Tokerud made the decision to purchase a 1904 adobe house in 1999, it was with the idea of renovating it and making it her main Marfa residence. It shared the lot with a building that Tokerud considered a tear-down: a 550-square-foot pink stucco frame house that was in such bad shape she didn't even set foot inside until weeks after her purchase was made. The former rental had no architectural appeal and was further burdened by a floor plan that revealed a direct view of the toilet from the front door.

But Tokerud realized she could renovate the little house to live in while she remodeled the main house; after that, the frame house could become her guesthouse. She collaborated with fellow Houstonian—now fellow Marfan—George Sacaris, an artist and designer with architectural training who works mainly in metal and is Tokerud's frequent associate in design projects. Tokerud wanted everything to be simple, white, and easy to maintain, so she and Sacaris gutted the dwelling and began to reconfigure the space. They discovered oak flooring and a perfectly preserved longleaf pine ceiling that had been the underside of the original roof. They saved the pitched tin roof, a recent improvement.

To give the tiny house a sense of spaciousness, Sacaris built steel-framed wood decks that extend from each of the three doors leading outside. Tokerud found a pair of antique French doors, which she used for the front entrance, and Sacaris built a pivoting five-by-seven-foot glass-and-steel door for the dining area. The simple third door opens from the kitchen onto a back deck and dining pavilion where Tokerud hosts parties and shows movies.

The house was essentially a little box, so the two designers set out to alter its undistinguished facade. Sacaris fashioned galvanized tin bump-outs for the bedroom and the shower, each with a ceiling of glass reinforced with a wire grid. The effect at night is magical. "I can look up at the stars at night when I'm in bed," says Tokerud, "or at the sky when I shower."

The designer used the color white extensively in the house—only one wall in the living room is covered in another hue, the same gray stucco that Tokerud spread on the exterior walls. She accentuates the light/dark contrast with a slit of a floor-to-ceiling window that admits a sliver of morning light. The architectural gesture offers the day's first glimpse of Marfa's legendary light.

In the living room, left, a David Fulton Plexiglas chair and a Christian Liaigre chaise serve as an antidote to the circa 1904 house's rustic underpinnings. Metal artist George Sacaris built the base for the pine dining table, above, which was formerly a Mexican door.

George Sacaris created an oversize, pivoting
metal door for the dining room; it allows cooling
breezes to flood the space.

A bump-out in the bedroom creates enough room for a bed with a fine view of the stars at night. This pavilion is connected to the little white house by an ipe-wood deck topped by an arbor. Tokerud uses the pavilion's interior wall as a movie screen. Her partner, Rick Houser, created all the millwork throughout the house and pavilion.

Ranch on the Horizon

The landscape around Marfa can seem inhospitable to anything man-made, which was one of the main challenges Houston architect Carlos Jiménez faced when he designed a residence for Houston decorative arts gallery owner Lynn Goode and her husband at the time, attorney Tim Crowley, in 2002. The 8,000-square-foot, single-story ranch house sits on the crest of more than two thousand acres and overlooks hectares of desert a few miles southwest of town.

The gleaming structure—now owned by Lindsay and Ford Smith—is isolated in the vastness, an intimidating reality that Jiménez negotiated by surrounding the Z-shaped building with a series of courtyards and patios. By framing the outside spaces instead of shutting out the landscape, these individual points for contemplation serve as buffers between the elegance of the house and the severity of the environment. Austin-based landscape designer Mark Word worked with Jiménez to establish an exterior architecture of subtle boundaries that would ease the environmental shock of entering and exiting the house. Word began by planting the motor court, entry patio, garden patio, and a strip around the perimeter of the house with drought-tolerant plants that get progressively more lush as they get closer to the swimming pool.

The house is constructed with intentionally modest materials such as light-gauge steel and galvanized gridiron of the type used in strip malls, and yet the building makes a stunning impression. In this unexpected context, the building materials read as special, if not downright precious. The effect is unexpectedly poetic in the way it establishes spatial resonance with the environment, a result of the graciousness embedded in Jiménez's design. The house's plan is straightforward: an elongated sequence of five linear wings that attach to each other on the perpendicular—with one exception—to form a compound. Two bedroom wings extend from a central rectangle where cooking, dining, and gathering happen. Projecting out diagonally from the point where the master bedroom wing and the central rectangle meet, the living room juts into the landscape with a window wall that acts like a viewfinder for the outside world.

While this is a dwelling that only exists in its built form because of the exterior landscape, it is also very much a private place with a distinct interior presence. Jiménez has made sure of that by enriching the rooms with light and varying its sources for constant changes in nuance throughout the day. A skylight in the front entrance illuminates the core of the house; windows in the dining room frame views of the horizon; and a double-height, north-facing window in the living room showcases the Fort Davis Mountains. The effect, especially at dawn and dusk, is intended to create a phenomenal and intimate exposure to the region's exceedingly clear atmosphere. The variations of light on the interior extrapolate the more-intense version outside; one of the most pleasing aspects of this house is its ability to allow engagement with the challenging environment while providing refuge from it. The result is a connectedness that's both exciting and comforting, a reinforcement of both material provocation and of aesthetic satisfaction.

Architect Carlos Jiménez designed this house
to help residents and visitors to feel safely
cosseted amid the sometimes agoraphobia-
inducing grandeur of the Marfa landscape. A
skylight in the entrance, for example, previous
pages, illuminates the core of the house
with Marfa light while shutting out the view
momentarily, as a respite. Brave windows in the
dining room and living room, however, frame
majestic views of the horizon. The cozy library
then again focuses on creature comforts.

Luxurious details in the master bedroom and
bath provide a textural resonance to nature's
wildness that gives this very private dwelling
a rich and civilized presence.

Outside spaces serve as buffers between the refined elegance of the house and the wild severity of the environment. Austin-based landscape designer Mark Word worked with Jiménez to establish an exterior architecture of intuitive boundaries to ease the shock felt when moving between the domestic sphere and the desert beyond.

Downtown

Vernacular

Houston-based interior designer Marlys Tokerud visited Marfa for the first time in 1998, but not the last. "I couldn't stay away," she says. A year and a half later, Tokerud saw a white stucco adobe house for sale near downtown. She purchased the 1904 dwelling, intending to restore it as her own residence. The house, just north of the railroad tracks that cut through the middle of town, wasn't quite ready for a new owner—the square building had been the longtime home of two sisters who were raised in it and who had remained in it throughout their lives, so some updates were necessary. Evidence—such as an antique chicken coop in the backyard—of long lives lived out in one place was still there.

"The house has been here for a hundred years," says Tokerud, "and I wanted to keep as much of the charming parts of that as I could." Many elements of the little house were special to her, such as the 10-foot-high ceilings, the 14-inch walls, and the painted wood doors—Tokerud kept them all and left remnants of the original paint showing. But some things couldn't stay, such as a ramshackle sleeping porch. Drainage on the lot was also a problem and had contributed to deterioration of the adobe house. Tokerud's partner Rick Houser created a winding drainage ditch disguised as a rock-filled dry creek bed that meanders through the middle of the corner lot. It separates the main house from the 550-square-foot guesthouse and an attached pavilion the couple built for showing outdoor movies and hosting big dinners for family and friends.

During the renovation process, Tokerud and Houser discovered longleaf pine floors that had been damaged by a long-ago fire and covered over with a new pine floor. Neither was salvageable, so Houser cut the longleaf pine into pieces that were used elsewhere in the house. Not long after the couple finished renovating, however, another fire broke out in the kitchen. The needed repairs offered an opportunity for upgrades, such as plaster walls and multiple coats of a glossy paint on the ceiling. Tokerud also added track lighting that's discreetly recessed into the ceiling. Houser built a kitchen island out of half a bowling lane imported from El Paso; he also built all the cabinets in the house and brought in industrial lighting from his Houston woodworking shop. Metal fabricator George Sacaris, who often works with Tokerud on other projects, made steel thresholds and baseboards for the house, a sturdy grounding for the straightforward décor.

Pieces by local artists or that are endowed with local significance grace the home throughout. The cloud painting in the living room is by Michael Roch and the photo in the dining room of oil wells and drills is by Joe Adams. In the kitchen, a collection of painted metal bar trays lines the wall across from the island.

A horse trough serves as a tub in the master bath, left, where vintage blue tequila bottles line a concrete shelf lit by a slit window in the plaster walls. Rick Houser takes a minute to shine his boots on a bench outside this century-old adobe house's kitchen, above.

Tumbling   Tripartite

When Suzanne and Tom Dungan moved to Marfa from Houston, they left a subtropical environment behind in favor of the extremes of the desert. The couple had been living in an aluminum-coated, galvanized steel house designed by architect Cameron Armstrong, who is known for design solutions tailored to climate. The Dungans engaged him again for their new house, which sits on the crest of a hill and is sited to overlook the broad horizon to both the east and west. When thinking about how the structure might evolve, Suzanne asked: "What would our house look like if we took three of Donald Judd's boxes and tumbled them down the hill?" The resulting building is composed of three sections that stair-step gently down the slope—the bedrooms are on the highest part of the grade and the entry and kitchen welcome guests midway, who may then step down into the living room.

The 2,400-square-foot dwelling is composed of E-Crete blocks—a lightweight, cost-effective, durable, and fire-resistant material that's easy to cut and shape and that doesn't disintegrate in the harsh West Texas environment. It visually resembles adobe, the building material of choice in this part of the world a century ago, but is much less fragile and requires very little maintenance. Prominent steel beams form the support structure of the house. Inside, concrete floors keep things cool in the summer but are warmed by radiant heat in the winter. The whitewashed pine ceiling extends out to create a substantial terrace that adds another 1,800 square feet to the living space and is a destination for parties, sky-watching, and bird-watching.

The Dungans brought many pieces from their art collection with them when they first moved to Marfa in 2004; it took four years for their current residence to be finished, but the wait for the double-height walls in the living room that were intended to provide ample display opportunities for their largest pieces was worthwhile. Most interior walls are a gallery white, accented by stacked and pressed bamboo panels that infuse the entry and kitchen with warmth and subtle pattern. Works on display includes pieces by Jeff Elrod, Tad Griffin, Susan Whyne, and Terry Winters, but the wall of windows open to the sunrise, mountain ranges, and the drama of the land's constant interactions of light, clouds, and earth show clearly that the view was also always intended to feature as a major work of art.

This house's prominent steel frame sets the tone for modern art and furniture. Above the hide-covered Le Corbusier lounge, previous pages, is a work by Marfa-based Jeff Elrod. A painting by Austin-based Susan Whyne hangs over the fireplace, next to a black-and-white abstract by Tad Griffin. In the entry, above, a Saarinen Tulip table is illuminated by one of two Frank Gehry fiber pendants—the other hangs over the French library table that doubles as a dining table, right. The owners purchased the Naugahyde-upholstered dining chairs at a sale at Sul Ross State University in nearby Alpine.

Suzanne Dungan paired two love seats by artist Michael Tracy in front of the fireplace on the 1,800-square-foot terrace, site of much sky-watching and bird-watching. The whitewashed pine ceiling extends through the interior and out over the terrace, visually expanding the sense of living space.

219

The Zen of Adobe

King Grossman could have turned right or left off Highway 59 one day as he was leaving Houston, but as fate would have it he veered left and headed west with no particular destination in mind. The writer had just finished the first draft of a novel and needed a place to polish it up. "I took the scenic route," Grossman says, "and ended up in Marfa." He and his wife, Lisa Leggett-Grossman, had visited West Texas just once before, for a family reunion in Fort Davis. King stayed a week—long enough to convince him he should buy a studio in Marfa where he could work. Lisa soon joined him.

Fate intervened again. After a Sunday service at St. Paul's Episcopal Church near the courthouse, the couple noticed a white, Zenlike house just on the other side of the street. A friend told them later in the day about a house they should see—the very same one they had remarked earlier. Although the adobe-block, 1,800-square-foot, one-bedroom dwelling wasn't for sale, the Grossmans took note. "We called the owner a year later," says Lisa, "and he'd just put the house on the market. We were living there thirty days later."

The century-old adobe building is known locally as "Barbara Hill's first house," a tribute to the Houston-based architectural designer whose edgy minimalism perfectly complements Marfa's gestalt. It had previously been used as both a lawyer's office and a beauty parlor when Hill purchased it as a weekend retreat. The former gallery owner originally thought that it didn't need any work. "A year later," she says, "I had torn everything out." That included a concrete-block sunroom in back, decorative wrought-iron columns in front—and various walls, windows, and ceilings. In place of a warren of small rooms with walls clad in imitation wood paneling, Hill decided to create three airy spaces.

Preserving the original adobe walls, however, had been a priority. The benefits of adobe are tangible: it makes a room warm in the winter and cool in the summer, not to mention that eighteen-inch-thick walls muffle sound well. To keep the adobe in place without the stability of many interior walls to support it, Hill and engineer Dan Ray of Alpine turned to steel beams. A nearly 50-foot-long, heavy-duty I-beam extends right through the center of the living room's pitched ceiling. As a counterbalance, two more-delicate-looking steel rods stretch across the room—and function as stylish as well as necessary structural elements.

Perhaps as important as architectural integrity was Hill's insistence on proportion in the house. "I rearranged the windows," she says about the tall rectangular openings in the living room that mimic the shape of the passage to the bedroom on the opposite side of the space. The walls that remain are now swathed in a luminous white plaster by American Gypsum that bestows total serenity on the spaces. Hill also decorated with the precision of a curator, so the previous owner and the Grossmans gladly retained her selections—including an accessory that Hill may have forgotten about. "She left her toothbrush," says Lisa. "We still have it, in case she ever wants to come back and stay overnight."

Two delicate-looking steel rods stretch across both edges of the room's width—these necessary structural elements are much stronger than they look and give the adobe lateral support. The hay bale coffee table is by The Art Guys, and a pair of Charles and Ray Eames sofas flank the table.

A long French work table now makes an inviting
dining table—a signature eclectic and surprisingly
scaled hallmark by designer Barbara Hill. Blackened
steel cabinets are a dramatic counterpoint to the
luminous white plaster walls throughout.

Hill's insistence on harmony and proportion
in the house ensured architectural integrity for
the interior spaces. She repositioned the tall,
rectangular living room windows to align with
the similarly tall rectangular door to the bedroom
on the other side of the room, for example. Floors
throughout are whitewashed pine.

Sky   Watch

It took Jean Landry and Richard Bullock all of forty minutes to fall in love with Marfa. The husband and wife work in the movie industry—he is a boom operator and dialogue recordist and she is a set designer—and until 2011 they lived in Los Angeles. At the prompting of Landry's mother and father, both architects in Dallas, the couple stopped for two nights in Marfa over Christmas seven years ago, on their way to visit her parents. "They thought we might like it," says Landry.

Due to the holiday, the town was empty. "There was nothing going on—it was totally quiet. Dead empty," recalls Landry. She and Bullock walked to the edge of Waco Street, and began asking themselves, "What is it with this place? It just feels so good here." The two big-city dwellers were smitten, but really only considered Marfa as a retirement option—thirty years hence. In fact, determined not to give in to their intuitive desire to move to Marfa, they returned to Los Angeles and started looking for a house to buy. "We bid on ten houses," says Landry. "We even bid on a house we didn't like—every bid fell through." Tired of the competitiveness of the Los Angeles real estate market, the couple returned to Marfa for a week.

The timing of the visit, however, couldn't have been worse. It was 2011 and the Rock House fire was raging. One of the fastest-moving wildfires in the state's history, it burned for twenty-eight days and ravaged 315,000 acres from Marfa to north of Fort Davis. When they arrived, Marfa was choked with smoke. But instead of deterring the couple, the disaster made them look on the town sympathetically. "It influenced us," she says. "We were impressed by the community—everyone came together and helped the fire department." So it was the

people as much as the mythic allure of the landscape that cemented their growing love for Marfa. "We got the idea to look for land," she says. "I'd always wanted my parents to design a house for me—but then we decided to look for a house in town." On a whim, they made an offer on a renovated one-bedroom, one-bath adobe house in town, and the offer was accepted. "Within a month, we moved to Marfa," says Landry.

The 1930s-era adobe house had been renovated by Stephen Bryan of Alpine, who was responsible for the bedroom-bath addition in the back and for enclosing a courtyard outside the bedroom. At the time they bought the house, the yard was mostly dirt. The couple hired landscape architect Jim Martinez—who they met at a game night he hosts semiregularly—to landscape the front yard, which is now a minimalist scene of gravel and an asymmetric smattering of sculptural succulents. As so often happens in Marfa, relatives of the original owner are still around. The sister lives across the street.

Although they don't have a direct view of the desert horizon from their house, Landry and Bullock enjoy another kind of view, one for which Marfa is equally famous. "We spend a lot of time in our courtyard," she says, "where we watch how the fence frames the clouds. It's all about the sky here. I could look at it all day long." She particularly enjoys watching storms approach and appreciates the newfound awareness she has acquired of the outside world. "It's fascinating to be more connected to the landscape," she says. The couple's lives are richer in other ways, too. "Our social and cultural lives are so much more active and richer here than they were in Los Angeles," she says. "It's so much easier, and there's virtually no excuse not to do something."

This 1930s-era adobe house had been recently renovated when the current owners bought it; it notably featured a bedroom-bath addition in the back and this enclosed courtyard outside the bedroom. The yard was mostly dirt, though, so the couple hired landscape architect Jim Martinez to landscape the front yard, previous pages, which is now a minimalist stage for a variety of sculptural succulents.

Jean Landry is partial to Scandinavian furniture, candles, and fabrics, and has decorated the house with her finds. She has also taken advantage of the presence of tumbleweeds by creating and selling Marfa Tumbleweed Lights, one of which hangs in the couple's living room.

The room formerly used as
a kitchen was in such bad
shape when builder Steve
Bryan renovated the house
that he had to tear it out; now
the galley kitchen links the
original house to the master
suite addition. Bryan creates
moments for vignettes, like this
arrangement of art and objects.

Adobe brick walls in the bedroom addition
are a rustic countermeasure to the smooth
white adobe walls in the original part of the
house. Concrete floors and a pine ceiling in the
bedroom, however, continue the aesthetics of the
original house into this space.

To Charles, who was there every step of the way

Acknowledgments

This is a book about private lives. Because of that we are indebted to the people who opened up their homes to us, as well as to the imaginative supporters who directed us to creative friends whose houses they thought would be right for this book. They were usually right, and thank goodness for that—their guidance helped us capture the essence of a fascinating town by venturing into its most personal spaces.

Our book wouldn't have been possible without the help of Marlys Tokerud, Kristin Bonkemeyer, Anne Adams, Jamey and Constance Holt-Garza, Tom and Suzanne Dungan, Barbara Hill, Julie Speed and Fran Christina, King Grossman and Lisa Leggett-Grossman, Jim Martinez and Jim Fissel, Michael Phelan, Vilis Inde and Tom Jacobs, Liz Lambert, Laszlo Thorsen-Nagel, Jean Landry and Richard Bullock, Terry Nowell, Larry and Laura Doll, Michael Barnard, Bill Aylor, Lindsay and Ford Smith, Linda and Don Shafer, David Lanman, Tim Crowley, Jason Archer, JD DiFabbio, Ginger Griffice, Jenn Dunn, Matt Genitempo, and Scott and Kelly Ferguson.

Thanks especially to our assistants Hayden Spears and Allen Corralejo and to our family and extended family: Charles Lohrmann, Ruth Smith, Tommy, Beverly, and Avery Dunn, and Sarah Weinstein. Special thanks to our editor, Stacee Lawrence, whose enthusiastic advocacy gave us a better and more beautiful book than we had dreamed possible. We are particularly grateful to Cody Haltom, whose intelligent, imaginative, and virtuosic design elevates both the message of the book and its intent to a level that a special place like Marfa deserves.

Copyright 2016 The Monacelli Press

All rights reserved.
Published in the United States by The Monacelli Press

Library of Congress Control Number 2016941805
ISBN: 978-1-58093-473-2

Printed in China
Designed by Cody Haltom

1 3 5 7 9 10 8 6 4 2
First Edition

The Monacelli Press
236 West 27th Street
New York, New York 10001

www.monacellipress.com